My Book of
Life Cycles

by Camilla de la Bédoyère

QEB

QEB Publishing

Copyright © QEB Publishing 2014

Designer: Andrew Crowson
Editor: Ruth Symons

First published in the US in 2014 by
QEB Publishing
3 Wrigley, Suite A
Irvine, CA 92618

www.qed-publishing.co.uk

A CIP record for this book is available from the
Library of Congress.

ISBN 978 1 60992 634 2

Printed in China

Words in **bold** are
explained in the
glossary on page 60.

Contents

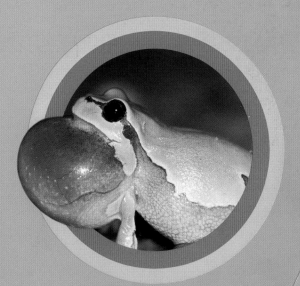

What is a life cycle?

The way that animals begin life, grow, and reproduce is called a life cycle.

When an animal begins its life we say it has hatched, or has been born. Young animals eat, grow, and explore the world.

⋁ When chicks hatch they are small and fluffy. They look very different from adult chickens.

1

⋀ **Butterflies lay eggs, which hatch into caterpillars.**

2

⋀ **Caterpillars eat all day and grow bigger and bigger.**

A butterfly experiences many stages during its life cycle.

⋁ The adult butterfly spreads its wings, ready to fly.

4

>> A pupa forms around the caterpillar and it changes into a butterfly.

3

The story of a frog

⌄ Female frogs lay eggs in the spring.

A frog is an **amphibian**. It spends part of its life in water, and part of its life on land.

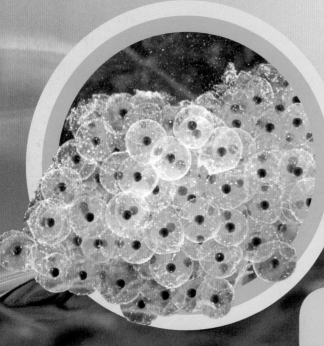

« Inside each egg, a new tadpole **is growing.**

Amphibians lay their eggs
in water and after a few
weeks the eggs hatch.

Tiny tadpoles

Tadpoles are tiny when they hatch, but they grow quickly.

Each tadpole has a long tail, which it uses to swim. It has feathery **gills** on either side of its head. These allow the young tadpole to breathe underwater.

⌃ **A frog spends the first two stages of its life cycle in the water.**

⌄ At first, tadpoles eat small water plants. Later, they will eat pond animals.

« Tadpoles grow faster when they live in warm water with plenty of food.

9

The big change

When they are about seven weeks old, tadpoles begin to change into frogs.

First, they grow back legs. A few weeks later, their gills disappear. Then they swim to the surface to breathe air. Their tails begin to shrink and their front legs grow.

3

2

1

^ As its legs grow longer, the tail grows shorter.

^ The tadpole's back legs grow first.

^ Then its front legs begin to grow.

4

⋎ By the time it is 12 weeks old, the tiny frog is about 3 centimeters long.

≪ Tadpoles are called froglets as soon as their tail disappears.

Adult life

Adult frogs spend most of their time on land. They hunt for insects, slugs, and worms.

>> **Frogs** hibernate **in the winter, when there is little food to eat, and the weather is cold.**

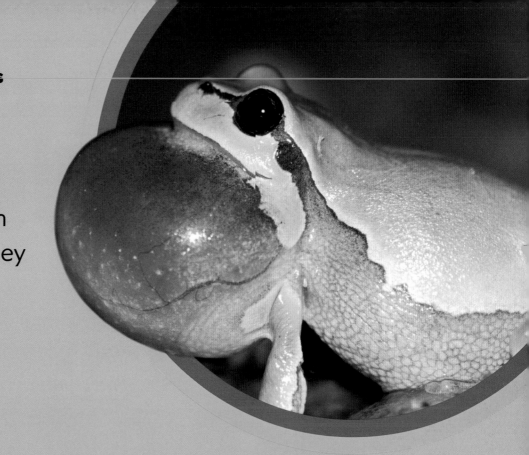

>> **Male tree frogs croak loudly.**

In spring, frogs return to the pond where they were born. Soon the story of the life cycle will begin again.

The story of a butterfly

A butterfly is a type of **insect**. Insects have three pairs of legs, making six legs altogether.

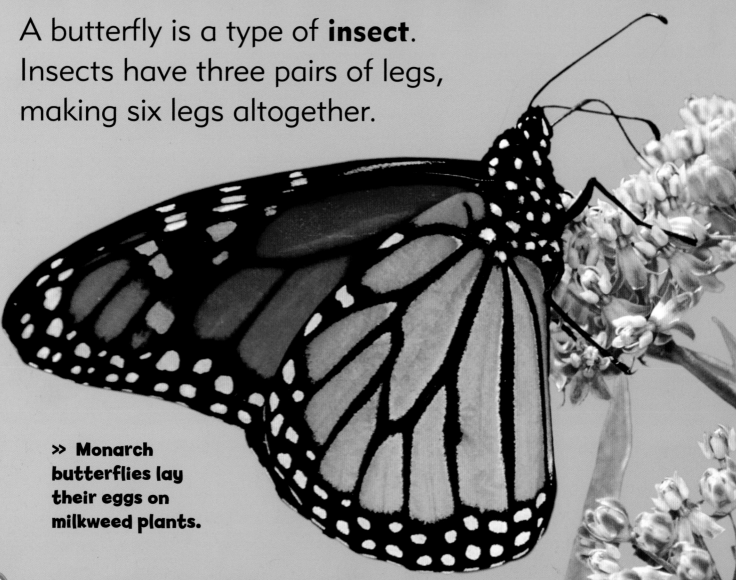

>> Monarch butterflies lay their eggs on milkweed plants.

In spring, a female butterfly searches for somewhere safe to lay her eggs. She lays them under leaves. The eggs stick to the leaves and are hidden from view.

⌃ Different types of butterflies lay different shaped eggs. These are monarch butterfly eggs.

« When the eggs hatch, the caterpillars start to eat right away.

15

The eggs hatch

About a week later, the eggs hatch, and a tiny yellow caterpillar comes out of each one.

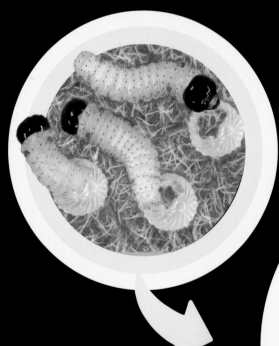

⋎ **Monarch caterpillars have stripes. This warns animals that they are** poisonous.

As a caterpillar grows, it sheds its skin, revealing new skin underneath. This is called **molting**.

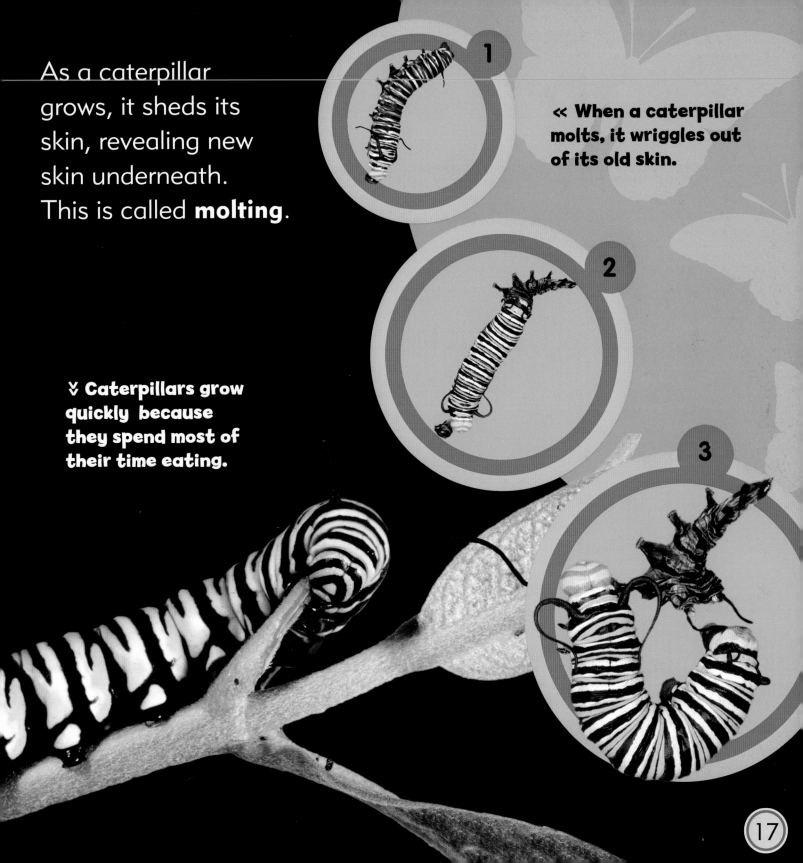

1

« When a caterpillar molts, it wriggles out of its old skin.

2

⌄ Caterpillars grow quickly because they spend most of their time eating.

3

Transformation

After about 14 days, a caterpillar is ready to change into a **pupa**. This is the next stage of its life cycle.

1

2

Pupa

« The caterpillar makes a silk thread, and uses it to hang from a leaf.

A caterpillar molts one last time, then it turns into a pupa. Inside the pupa, the caterpillar gradually changes. After about two weeks, the pupa cracks open and the butterfly crawls out.

⌄ **The butterfly spreads its wings so they can dry.**

3

4

⌃ **The butterfly has to rest for a few hours before it can fly.**

A long journey

As the summer comes to an end, monarch butterflies start an amazing journey, called a **migration**.

« Millions of monarch butterflies spend the winter resting on trees.

Monarch butterflies fly to warmer places. The journey can cover thousands of miles and takes more than two months.

>> Male and female monarchs look similar, but males have small dark spots on their back wings.

21

The story of a penguin

Emperor penguins live in big groups called **colonies**. Their home is in the Antarctic, which is at the bottom of our planet Earth.

>> **Males and females can call to each other. The sound they make is called a bray.**

At the start of winter, emperor penguins meet on sheets of ice to find their mate.

>> **Male and female penguins stay together.**

⋏ **Penguin chicks are gray and fluffy.**

Laying an egg

Emperor penguins do not build nests. They carry their eggs instead.

The female lays a single egg. The male uses his beak to push it onto his feet. He has a bare patch of skin on his belly, called a brood patch. He lays this skin over the egg.

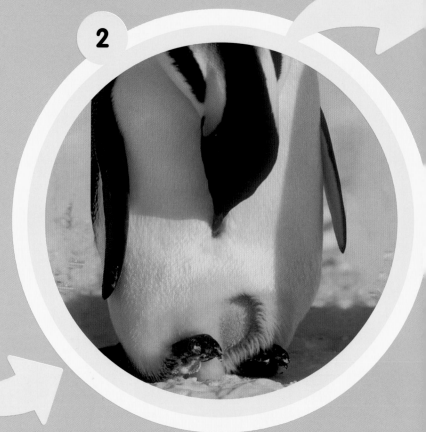

« The egg has a strong shell on the outside.

⌃ The brood patch keeps the egg warm.

>> The egg is on the male's feet, where it will be kept warm.

3

The long walk

The males look after the eggs and the females walk back to the sea. The long walk takes four weeks.

>> The female penguins catch lots of fish and fill their stomachs with food.

<< The males do not eat while the females are away. They huddle together to keep warm.

After feeding, the female walks back to the colony and finds her mate. Now the male can give the egg to the mother. He walks to the sea to find food.

<< **The female takes her egg from the male.**

The egg hatches

The chick breaks out of the shell. It sits on its mother's feet to keep warm.

1

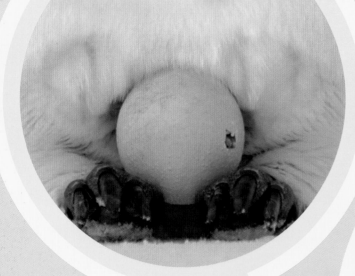

⌃ **The shell begins to crack open.**

2

>> **The chick comes out of the shell.**

The father comes back from the sea. He has a stomach full of food. The parents take turns feeding the chick. They keep it warm and safe.

3

⌃ **The parents feed the chick with food from their stomach.**

≫ **The chick stays with its parents.**

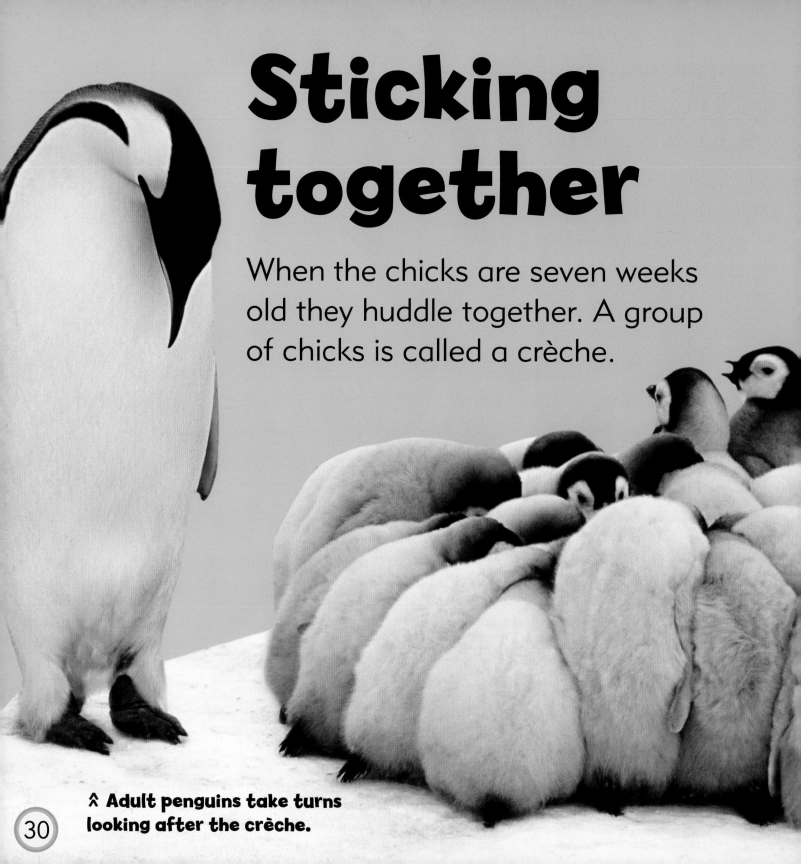

Sticking together

When the chicks are seven weeks old they huddle together. A group of chicks is called a crèche.

⌃ **Adult penguins take turns looking after the crèche.**

As they grow, the chicks get new feathers. Soon they will look like their parents. When they are adults, the young penguins will lay their own eggs. The life cycle will begin again.

>> Chicks lose their fluffy feathers as new feathers start growing.

>> Young penguins know how to swim. Their parents do not have to teach them.

The story of a sea horse

A sea horse is a type of fish. It has **scales**, a tail, and **fins**.

Fins

Tail

« Sea horses have a long tail and tiny fins.

During **courtship**, male and female sea horses dance for each other. The sea horses wrap their tails around each other, and swim together.

⌄ **A baby sea horse is called a fry.**

Life begins

After female sea horses lay their eggs, the males look after them for up to six weeks.

1

2

« The eggs of a sea horse are very small.

⌃ The male keeps the eggs in a special pouch on his belly.

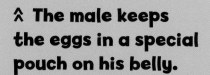

Some sea horses give birth to five fry at a time. Others can have hundreds. As soon as the fry are ready, they swim away.

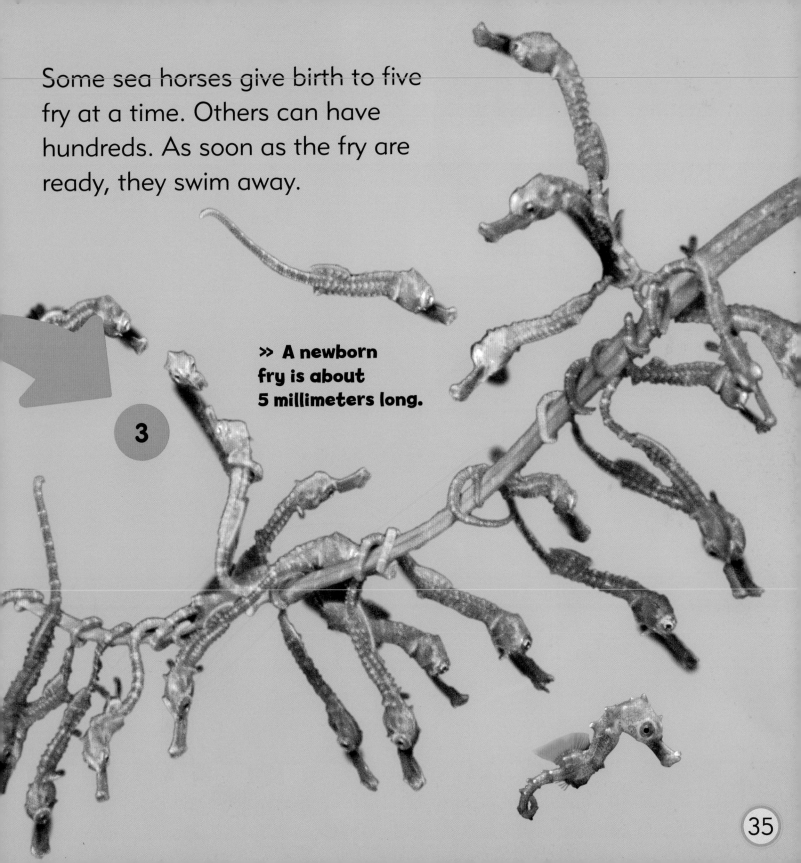

>> A newborn fry is about 5 millimeters long.

3

Growing up

Hatchlings are very small when they are born but will grow bigger quickly.

⌄ Fry eat small sea animals such as brine shrimp.

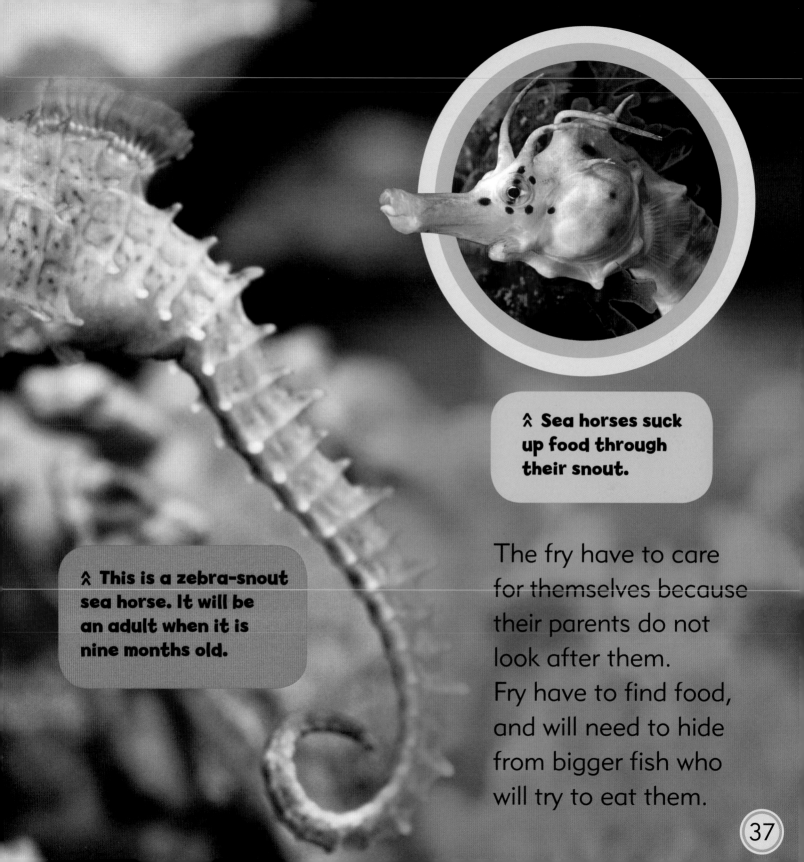

∧ Sea horses suck up food through their snout.

∧ This is a zebra-snout sea horse. It will be an adult when it is nine months old.

The fry have to care for themselves because their parents do not look after them. Fry have to find food, and will need to hide from bigger fish who will try to eat them.

How sea horses live

There are more than
30 types of sea horses.
Most sea horses live
in warm, shallow water.

« The best place to
watch sea horses is
in the wild.

Sea horses are not good swimmers.
They wrap their curly tail around plants,
so the water does not drag them away.

⌄ **Leafy sea dragons can hide easily in seaweed and other plants.**

⌃ **Sea horses have very flexible tails.**

The story of a shark

A shark is a kind of fish. Young sharks are called pups. All pups begin life as eggs.

∨ Sharks are excellent swimmers. Their fins help them swim and change direction.

« Some pups are covered with patterns that help them to hide. This is called camouflage.

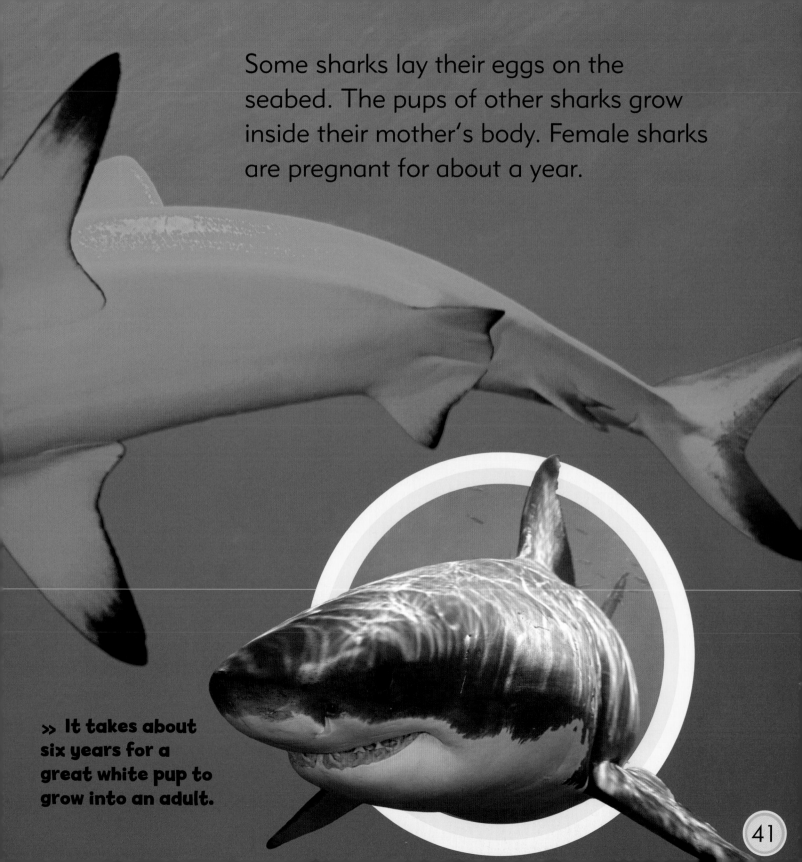

Some sharks lay their eggs on the seabed. The pups of other sharks grow inside their mother's body. Female sharks are pregnant for about a year.

>> It takes about six years for a great white pup to grow into an adult.

Laying eggs

Female swell sharks must find a safe place to lay their eggs.

Each egg is held in a rubbery case called a mermaid's purse.

The case protects the pup growing inside it.

1

⌃ Inside an egg case there is a tiny shark pup and white yolk.

2

≪ At three months, the shark pup's tail has grown longer.

3

≫ After seven to ten months the swell shark pup is ready to hatch.

4

⌄ An adult swell shark can grow nearly 4 feet long.

How sharks live

Sharks swim silently through the sea, searching for food to eat.

⌄Great white sharks can grow up to 20 feet in length.

<< Whale sharks are the largest fish in the world. They feed on tiny animals called krill.

>> Hammerhead sharks have huge heads.

Great white sharks hunt seals and other fish. They attack with lightning speed and have teeth as sharp as razors.

The story of a chicken

A hen is a female chicken, a rooster is a male chicken and a chick is a baby chicken.

« When a rooster wants to mate, he crows loudly.

A hen's eggs will only grow into chicks if she has already mated with a rooster.

>> When the hen has laid her eggs she sits on them to keep them warm. This is called brooding.

<< Inside the egg, the chick gets food from the yellow yolk and the clear albumen.

The eggs hatch

After growing for about three weeks, the young chicks are ready to break out of their eggs.

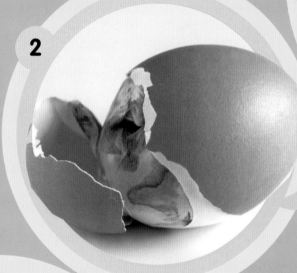

3

2

1

<< **The chick chips a hole all around the shell.**

Each chick has a sharp point on their top beak, called an egg-tooth. The chick uses its egg-tooth to crack a hole in the shell and push its way out.

4

« The newly hatched chick cheeps loudly. It is tired and its feathers are wet.

⌄ Once their feathers have dried, chicks become fluffy.

5

Life as a chick

The hen looks after her newly hatched chicks. She keeps them warm under her wings.

∨ Newly hatched chicks stay close to their mother.

>> The chicks grow red, fleshy combs on top of their heads. The combs help them to keep cool.

⌄ Chicks and chickens like to scratch in the dirt for tasty worms or bugs to eat.

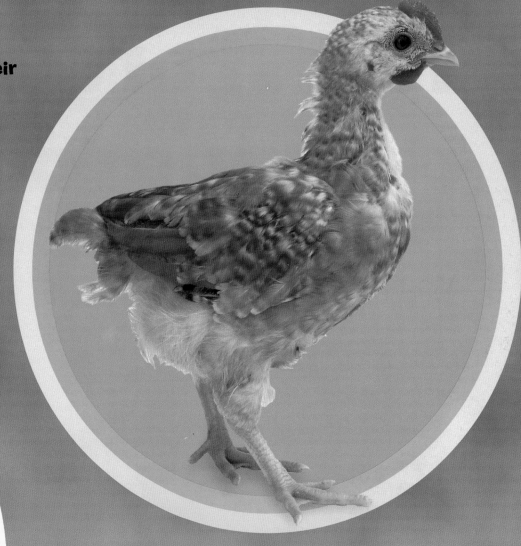

The chicks grow into adults in just a few months. Glossy feathers grow in place of the soft, fluffy feathers. Soon the young hens will start to lay eggs.

The story of a kangaroo

Kangaroos are **mammals**. Mammals have fur and give birth to babies, which they feed with milk.

>> When male kangaroos, called jacks, want to mate with females, they fight with one another.

Kangaroos belong to a group of mammals called **marsupials**. A marsupial mother has a special pouch. She keeps the baby in her pouch while it grows bigger.

⌃ A baby kangaroo is called a joey. When it is born, it is no bigger than a fingernail.

⌃ Kangaroos have long, strong legs perfect for jumping across Australia's wide grasslands.

Ready, set, grow!

As soon as a joey is born, it pulls itself up into its mother's pouch. Inside the pouch, it feeds, sleeps, and grows.

A joey is nearly five months old before it can open its eyes. Then it pushes its head out and looks around.

>> **The mother cleans her joey and the pouch by licking them with her long tongue.**

∧ For the first few months, the joey slowly grows bigger.

∧ A joey watches what goes on around it.

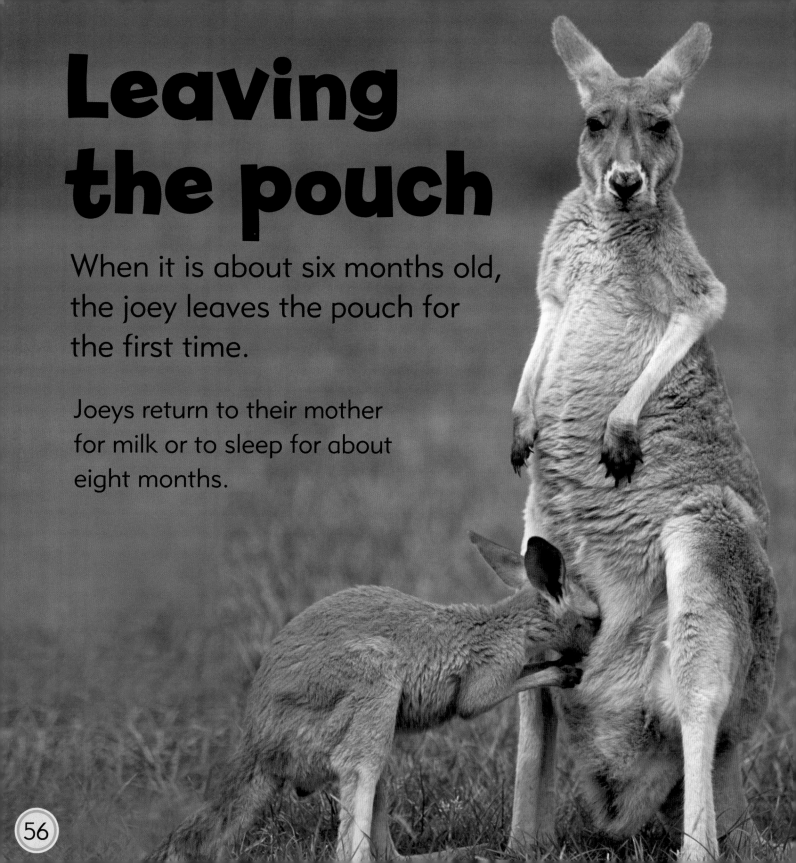

Leaving the pouch

When it is about six months old, the joey leaves the pouch for the first time.

Joeys return to their mother for milk or to sleep for about eight months.

≪ When a joey is scared, it stays safe in its mother's pouch.

≪ Although this joey is too big to get into the pouch, it still feeds on its mother's milk.

57

Adult life

Kangaroos live together in groups, called mobs. They spend much of their time eating.

∨ **Red kangaroo males have reddish fur, but females have gray fur.**

∧ **There are between two and ten kangaroos in a mob.**

Kangaroos graze on plants, such as grass. They can travel long distances in search of food and water.

⌃ When an adult kangaroo is scared, it quickly jumps to safety.

Glossary

albumen The white part inside an egg.

amphibian An animal that spends the first part of its life cycle in the water, and the second part mostly on land.

brooding When a hen sits on her eggs to keep them warm.

colony A group of animals that live together.

comb The soft, red skin on top of a chicken's head.

courtship When males and females are planning to mate.

fin Part of a fish's body that is used to swim.

gill Part of a fish or tadpole's body used to breathe underwater.

hibernate To spend the winter months in a kind of deep sleep.

insect A small animal with six legs. Butterflies are insects.

mammal An animal that has fur and feeds its young with milk.

marsupial A type of mammal that gives birth to very small young. Some marsupials keep their young safe in a pouch.

mate When a male and female come together and a new life starts to grow.

migration A long journey made by an animal.

molting When an animal sheds, or gets rid of, its old skin or feathers.

poisonous Harmful to eat.

pupa The life stage during which a caterpillar changes into an adult butterfly.

scales Hard little pieces of skin that cover a fish's body.

tadpole When a young frog hatches from its egg and lives all the time in water.

yolk Part of an egg that provides food for a growing animal.

Index

Photo credits

Alamy 23t Wayne Lynch / All Canada Photos, 38b blickwinkel, 38-39 Juniors Bildarchiv, 40bl Visual&Written SL, 41tr © David Fleetham / Alamy

Corbis 6l Martin B Withers / Frank Lane Picture Agency, 6-7 Craig Holmes / Loop Images, 20l Danny Lehman, 21br Darrell Gulin, 23b Kevin Schafer, 38-39 Specialist Stock, 45c Visuals Unlimited, 45r Visuals Unlimited, 52b Martin Harvey Gallo Images, 60t Darrell Gulin

FLPA 6-7 Derek Middleton, 7r Wil Meinderts / FN / Minden, Jef Meul / FN / Minden, 55tr Mitsuaki Iwago/Minden Pictures, 56bl Janet Finch, 59b Gerard Lenz

fotoLibra 59t Guenter Lenz

Getty 8-9 Jane Burton, 12-13 Christoph Burki, 22 Joseph van Os, 24l David Tipling, 31br Bill Curtsinger, 33br Science Faction, 34bl Georg Grall/National Geographic, 45t Alex Kerstitch, 47tr Dorling Kindersley, 49t Jane Burton, 49b GK Hart/Vikki Hart, 50-51 Klaus Nigge, 50-51c Babusi Octavian Florentin, 54b Art Wolfe, 56r Art Wolfe, 58-59 Frank Krahmer

Imagequestmarine.com 40-41 Masa Ushioda, 44-45 Andy Murch / V&W

Kuhnphoto.net 12 ©David Kuhn/Dwight Kuhn Photography

Naturepl.com 2 Fred Oliver, 10r Pete Oxford, 17l Thorsten Milse, 17r Thorsten Milse, 25c Fred Oliver, 28tl Fred Oliver, 28br Solvin Zankl, 42-43 Doug Perrine, 43t Doug Perrine, 44cr Jurgen Freund

NHPA 10l George Barnard, 10c George Barnard, 10t George Barnard, 11 Stephen Dalton, 16l Kitchin & V Hurst, 58 ANT Photo Library

OceanwideImages.com 34-35 Rudie Kuiter, 37tl Rudie Kuiter, 37b Rudie Kuiter, 39t Gary Bell

Photolibrary Group 1b Oxford Scientific, 1r David B Fleetham, 3 Markus Botzek, 34r Oxford Scientific, 13tr Markus Botzek, 14-15 Richard Day, 15t Earth Science Animals, 20-21 Radius Images, 25r Don Paulson / Superstock, 26l Frank Krahmer / Cusp, 26-27 Wayne Lynch, 27l Doug Cheeseman / Peter Arnold Images, 30-31 Konrad Wothe / Oxford Scientific, 32bl LOOK-foto, 32-33 Oxford Scientific, 34-35 Peter Arnold Images, 36 Oxford Scientific, 38bl Tips Italia, 39 Max Gibbs, 40bl Reinhard Dirscherl, 41r David B Fleetham, 43br David B Fleetham, 44-45 Richard Herrmann, 47bl Andre Maslennikov, 52-53 IFA Animals, 53tr Oxford Scientific (OSF), 54-55 Juniors Bildarchiv

Shutterstock 1, 4-5 jps, 5tr bcampbell65, 5b BMJ, 8c Thomas Mounsey, 14t Jacob Hamblin, 15b SF Photo, 16t Cathy Keifer, 16-17 Jacob Hamblin, 17t Cathy Keifer, 17c Cathy Keifer, 17r Cathy Keifer, 18l Cathy Keifer, 18r Cathy Keifer, 19l Laurie Barr, 19r Laurie Barr, 31tr BMJ, 40-41 Levent Konuk, 44bl Krzysztof Odziomek, 45tr frantisekhojdysz, 46 bl CVHB Photography, 48b Saied Shahin Kiya, 48c Saied Shahin Kiya, 48t Saied Shahin Kiya, 51tr Jozsef Szasz-Fabian, 55b Inc, 57 Satheesh Nair, 58-59 wizdata, 59tr Christopher Meder